INTRODUCTION

Life happens to us all and in one of my podcast episodes, I discussed the truth about entrepreneurship and how it is not for the faint at heart. All is well in our lives, as entrepreneurs when our businesses are profitable. But to get there, we burn both ends of the candle stick, late nights, early mornings, and many sacrifices, and we choose to stay the course. There are challenges with staying the course and the goals we are striving to accomplish. The struggles with managing anxiety and stress are prevalent.

So many times, we can get caught up in the winds of life that we forget about what got us to that transformation point. The struggles, challenges, mental anguish, and everything that would have us throwing in the towel.

Mental health is a topic that many discuss especially when it comes to one's personal life. However, many fail to share the challenges an entrepreneur goes through which weighs them down, feeling hopeless, anxious, depressed, and burned out.

I often think about how other business owners value their self-care. Do they recognize the effects on their wellbeing, set boundaries, etc? A part of our identity lies within the layers of the success we have. Whenever that success of any kind is threatened it can leave one spiraling down a rabbit hole of negative thoughts and emotions that in some cases drives our actions internally and externally.

The 2020 pandemic caused a lot of people to be still. They were faced with making tough decisions in their personal lives and within their businesses. Many had to abruptly stop business operations they spent years or even decades building. Employees were no longer employed and the big question of what's next I'm quite sure was on everyone's mind.

I must admit I was one of those entrepreneurs. In this book, I want to be transparent and real about mental healing and entrepreneurship. Entrepreneurship is not for the weak. You must know who you are and what you want while embarking on this journey, most importantly it is essential to be mentally, and physically prepared for it.

There is a beautiful side and the ugly one to entrepreneurship. Not too many people are willing to be vulnerable and transparent about it. But it is the vulnerability and transparency that helps one to overcome, and be honest with themselves, and during their openness; another person can be helped. On my journey of healing,

I have found several keys to managing mental wellness that has been helpful. I hope you will find this book to be empowered with the understanding that you are not alone. Everyone has a story with chapters still being written and here's my story about the ugly truth about entrepreneurship,

CHAPTER 1

Behind The Mask

At one point in my life when I was going through my divorce, someone told me to remove the mask. Being the strong woman, I have always been I thought to myself, what mask? That phrase had some value to it, and we walk around in life facing challenges without showing the weakness that stems from it. Masks are made to hide who or what is lurking behind them. We all have had the mask on; showing up one way while within we are in a different state of being.

The beginning of a thing usually isn't the start of it. There are small and subtle moments that we can manage without it bothering us, so the impact goes unnoticed. You are unbothered and able to move forward easily through faith and prayer. In entrepreneurship, there are so many layers of challenges we are faced with.

For startups, the challenges range from believing you can do it to the execution of the plan. Then they evolve into funding and gaining customers while your belief system is being tested. Of course, more challenges for start-ups exist and they can be different for everyone.

There's a thing about success. Success says you arrived and when that moment is challenged by adverse situations it tackles your mindset and your well-being is not so well. Depression sets in leaving you fighting yourself while taking the blows of external impacts. In accordance, with a 2019 Berkeley study on entrepreneurship health and wellness, "23% of entrepreneurs are asymptomatic". This means these entrepreneurs do not have a history of mental illness. The point is you don't have to have a mental illness to be mentally unhealthy.

Circumstances happen which affect your thought life and perception. Me, I don't have a history of mental illnesses in my family. Challenges and struggles have occurred in my life many times. From being a single mom raising my daughter, later getting married only to be divorced years later. Going back to school to complete my degrees while working full time, raising my daughter, and running a full-time business. Eventually experiencing a layoff after working for a company for 20 years.

Let's pause right here, as women we strive to be all and do all for everyone while maintaining our sanity. Some of us, value self-care moments to refresh and go back to the routine while others don't value it and get burned out. We strive to wear the Supergirl cape or Wonder Woman's crowns and bangles. But at the end of the day, while lying in our tubs with candles and a glass of wine. We unwind only by discovering the realization that we are only Human.

I can't forget about the men. Men, you have the weight of the world on your shoulders from being the provider of your home to being a high performer and overachiever.

You have to be superman to so many while neglecting your own needs.

Ok, back to my story. After my layoff in 2018, I moved my side business up to full-time entrepreneurship, I encouraged myself every minute and was diligent in going after major government and corporate contracts. For 2 years, I was successful in scaling to six figures. 2020 arrived, and this world was stricken with a pandemic our generations had never seen before. It was like, the movie "The Day the Earth Stood Still", we were in a complete shutdown and life changed for everyone. Many people lost loved ones, and jobs, and plenty of business owners lost their companies.

The impact was felt worldwide. My business' core profitability came from event contracts with corporations and the state/federal government. The event, tourism, and hospitality industries were hit the hardest. I faced myself during those two years. My money rapidly decreased, and I didn't know what to do. In all transparency, I believe in God and my faith lies with him, but I was on the edge and ready to throw in the towel. I was experiencing a place I had not been in before and coping was hard to grasp.

It does not take much to go from a sense of security to a sudden downward turn of events. Behind the mask was and is a comfortable place for every entrepreneur. So many will talk about their six and seven figures, but what did it take for them to get there; better yet to remain at that level? Removing the mask is something we are not ready for because it forces us to see our true selves.

CHAPTER 2

Entrepreneurship Is Not For The Weak

Many people think that owning a business is easy and it's not. If you are not a person that likes discipline and meeting goals; then entrepreneurship is not for you. The separation of your emotions and sensitivity is necessary for your business along with the daily choices you must make. It takes a lot of discipline to be a business owner whether you have a full-time or part-time endeavor.

There are many risks to take and for some the mental strain and challenges are overwhelming. This type of stress can reduce the capacity of a person having people thinking why they even started. But how do you combat that? What do you do?Let's face it, many entrepreneurs start a business out of a need or from a hobby. They might grow the business organically and without laying a true foundation through business planning.

Here's a nugget, the truth about a strong brand is in the strength of its business plan. Ok, how does this planning help with mental wellness is what you're probably asking? Thank you for the question, bringing peace through your business with proper planning minimizes the risk and alleviates stress.

"PERSISTANCE" ARTHUR LEE BURRIS JR.

FOUNDER & CEO OF PORTEIRO

WWW.PORTEIRO.COM

The first two years of the pandemic taught me so much about myself. Managing mental wellness is a real thing. And if you were already unstable in your thinking whether it was lack of confidence, any kind of trauma, fear, defeating thoughts and so much more; then the biggest risk you face is risking having a sound mind. Mental health is a slippery slope. It takes several or even one occurrences to impact your life tremendously.

Some entrepreneurs are dealing with emotional situations within their personal lives, so not all the trials are within the business, but those external circumstances weigh heavily on a business owner's mindset. I've been there and therefore I'm writing this book. There are keys to managing wellness that will help every entrepreneur to remain their sanity.

Keys To Managing
Mental Wellness

CHAPTER 3

Be Honest With Yourself

The first key to managing mental wellness as an entrepreneur is being honest with yourself about where you are.

There's such a facet built up around looking like you have it together. In my process, the most challenging part was watching what I worked hard on fall apart right in front of my eyes. As I mentioned in the introduction, I have been active in entrepreneurship for over 20 years. When I was laid off in 2018. I did not complete my plan for full-time entrepreneurship.

Yes, I had a plan. I was working on minimizing my expenses, being educated on acquiring government contracts, and increasing the position of my business so I could go full-time within my established timeline. One thing about being an event producer, you must be ready for the unexpected. However, in my personal life, I wasn't quite ready for the layoff. But what could I do about that? I chose to have a positive outlook and amped up my need to learn and execute a plan all at the same time for my business.

I strived to keep the distractions away that I knew would only impact my faith and my thinking. I believed in and applied the methods I learned with government contracting and I was successful in that area for two years.

Now because of the layoff and the job market didn't open up for a minority woman in her 40s with 20 years of professional experience and diverse skillsets, a Bachelor's in Business Management and Administration and a Master's in Management. I say this because the challenges you face do not care about your accolades

I was happy being a full-time entrepreneur and being in control. I set up systems and did everything correctly in terms of building my business. But like with so many others, I didn't see the pandemic coming that would halt my business operations. I found myself with my back up against the wall, me against me moment. Struggling with a part of me wanting to let go of all my hopes and dreams while the other part was screaming keep going. Navigating through a hard place is not easy and everything slaps you in the face.

I tried keeping the smile on my face, hope was barely alive, and staying in my bubble of faith was tough. Praying wasn't easy. In public or around friends and family I pretended to be ok; acting like I had everything under control. When in fact, I was caving on the inside from worry and distress. I attempted to function within other skill sets to bring in streams of income, but I was not mentally prepared to handle any additional tasks.

Questions of what's going to happen with my house, car, and dog. My mind was wrecked with infiltrating negative thoughts. What I look like with my daughter was the biggest one since I had been focused on building a legacy. I had to be honest with myself. I found myself being resentful for the poor decisions I made in the past.

I felt as if the results of those decisions were catching up with me. I regretted everything. Let's be real, how many of us have been in those resentful moments?

Self-awareness is important. Understanding what will make or break you. What keeps you going or what will take you under? Some people might be battling past trauma, ADD, attachment styles, or ADHD. Whatever it looks like to you when you look at yourself in the mirror is the place where you come face to face with yourself. This is the moment of honesty. You can lie to others, but not to yourself. For me, I was honest with myself, and it was an ugly moment.

Oftentimes, taking a step back from everything is required. You may have a family, and work a 9-5 while managing a business. Life happens, you have bills, family issues, illness, and burned out in a perfect world. You are built to handle so much and it will take a toll on your body just as much as your mind.

What are your takeaways from this chapter? Where are you with understanding the deep part of yourself? Take time and reflect. What challenges have you or are you facing that has you at a crossroads?

"STEADY PUSHING FORWARD" KARLONTY WALLACE
FOUNDER & CEO OF PAWSATIVE
WWW.PAWSPARTNERSHIPS.COM

Notes
CHAPTER 3

CHAPTER 4

Know Your Capacity

Knowing your capacity is an important key that establishing boundaries. As entrepreneurs, we are everything within and outside our businesses. Sometimes we can take on too much that we strive to operate from an empty glass with nothing being poured back in. Now I'm not saying don't be there for others. But be there for yourself just as much as you are for others.

Give from an overflowing glass, not an empty one. Between 2020 and 2021, I was at my limit, I was on the edge, and no one knew it. I was alone in something I didn't believe others could understand. I had always been the one to be there for everyone. When they asked, I would do or strive to do the best of my ability. As I sit back and think about it, I put myself behind so many times being a resource for others. I watch them grow from my advice, hard work on their behalf, or brief conversations.

Before the pandemic, I was working on several business development projects for others along with maintaining my business. During the pandemic, I was at a breaking point that I no longer had it in me to be there for others. I extended past a threshold; I never knew I had. I would tell people, "I don't have the capacity to handle anything outside of me right now", that even included tough conversations.

Knowing your capacity is a protective place, a boundary that keeps you within your limits. No matter how much we believe we can handle, we are made to only handle so much. And guess what?! It's ok to set that boundary. This is where I remain. It keeps me in a place of balance. What are your boundaries?

CHAPTER 5

Seek Help And Support

Mental health awareness is important for entrepreneurs. Like the popular UNICEF quote, " A mind is a terrible thing to waste", it is imperative to understand how delicate our minds are. Let's be clear, I'm not a clinical therapist, but as a business strategist that has been at the point of no return, I returned with a message. I am an entrepreneur who had experience. Once again, my business had been my sole income for 2 years. I went from thriving to surviving. Went from working with international corporations, celebrities, government contracting, and providing event service throughout the US; all for things to stop abruptly because of something that was outside of my control.

Your brain is an extravagant organ in the physical state but is also where the mental capacity of your mind lives. Protect it at all costs. Have you ever considered what the stories are for some homeless people? I used to work at Burger King when I was 19. There was a man from the surrounding neighborhood who was homeless and lost his grip on reality. He had enough in him to survive.

Those who knew him told me that he was once a professor who had a traumatic experience where he lost everything, his wife, and himself. All I saw was a man who came to Burger King every morning for coffee. His ability to cope was gone. He snapped. I mentioned this story to help you understand that there is a very thin line in the mental fabric of our being and how trauma affects people differently.

It's important to seek help and have a support system from your friends or family. If they are not enough, contact a certified therapist to talk to. This takes me back to the previous key value, "know your capacity" sometimes the weight is too much for you to handle. Operate from a place of wholeness.

I found myself in a position of needing help and I felt as if I was in survival mode. I felt like a failure and that my world was imploding on me. I've seen a lot of entrepreneurs battle life changes, family issues, and struggles within their businesses that they pull away. Some may have their ways of coping, but it's overwhelming and hard to maintain composure. As an entrepreneur, how many of you have felt like this?

KNOW YOUR CAPACITY!

CHAPTER 6

Confidence In Your Voice

It's ok to say no. People have not found the confidence in knowing that saying no helps you to stay on the task yourself. I know you have heard the saying you can't give from an empty well. Like in chapter 3 we talked about knowing your capacity. During my battle with myself in 2020 and 2021, I learned the value of saying no and I felt ok with it. I have a question for you. What keeps you from speaking up for yourself? If you have too much on your plate what keeps you from saying no, I am unable to, or unavailable?

I'll wait for you to think about it. Let's write it out:

_____
_____
_____
_____
_____
_____
_____
_____
_____
_____
_____
_____

Now what you wrote is for you to ponder over. The whole goal of this chapter is to help you find confidence in your voice. Once again as business owners we take on a lot, especially solopreneurs; we are the CEO, CFO, marketing director, and public relations, and if you have products to produce - you are also the developer. The list goes on, but we don't say no to ourselves either. Recognizing that you can't take on more work and having to outsource keeps us from burnout. There are times we will take on more clients than we can handle, and we risk underperformance. This only adds to more stress and overworked days.

This plays a part in our mental capacity to cope with sudden changes, challenges, increased business, and so forth. Being honest with ourselves is necessary. There's a term everyone uses now, "booked and busy", and this is glorified. Being busy without proper planning, having a system, a schedule, a team, or automation will only lead to burnout. Typically, when people get burned out, it's usually hard for them to regain strength and even the confidence to get back into the business.

In my case of being so overwhelmed, I couldn't show up to help anyone with a business or with their events. I was limited in my thinking, and I knew I would underperform. The best thing I could say for us all was no; I can't assist you. I have always been the type of person who loves showing up for other people. I love helping others, but I couldn't. In that experience, I understood the value of saying no. You must be at a place of knowing and having a balance. It is ok to be there for others, but not to a point of extending beyond your own mental and physical capacity. This is a good practice for us overachievers.

CHAPTER 7

Work-Life Balance

You hear everyone talk about having a work-life balance. You may wonder how you can do that with the hustle and bustle of your life. The question of "how can I" when you have a family to care for, a demanding 9-5, a business to run, and needing some quality for yourself. How can I do this without missing something? Then you go on to feel stressed while reading these sentences. **Calm down, take a deep breath, 3,2,1, breathe and breathe again.**

Now let's dig in. Having a work-life balance is not easy especially if you're wondering how much time to give to one thing. Some people can plan out their day perfectly, and others just take things as it comes. Work-life integration should be effortless as a common thing once you get used to it. It should be like breathing. Most importantly, you should also feel a peace along with what you do. Just knowing you can flow within a slight schedule to take time out for something is a goal to strive for. It takes practice, a schedule, and time management that's realistic for life itself.

Various things can happen without warning. It's life! You can plan to do something one day but can feel a little under the weather the next day. You take time to rest and then you are off to the race of playing catch up. The biggest lesson in this is understanding the power of Its ok. As well as ensuring that you stay on task with your responsibilities.

In the next chapter, we'll talk about setting up systems, but I want to focus on the balance and how achieving it reduces stress. Stress comes from chaos in your life whatever that looks like for you. Chaos can be as simple as not being organized, not working within a timeline, allowing laziness and procrastination to set in, or something big like the pandemic happening.

Let's be real about it, we find ourselves in those moments when we don't want to be productive, we want to hide, and we then fall behind. These life hacks talked about in this book will help you get on a path that reduces the noise in your life. Having a peaceful state of being even in busy times allows you to flow through it like a steam of water flowing thru the rocks. This is balance. Working in the event industry, you see your fair share of "moving pieces" that can keep you stressed if you allow it to.

I have found myself pulling away for a moment to breathe so I can continue to handle my tasks in providing an excellent event. Alleviating stress allows one to think clearly, being able to make quick and sensible decisions. It's the same in your day-to-day life as an entrepreneur. Although, the pandemic caused plenty of problems in my life; it also afforded me the time to think and regroup. While my business wasn't fully operational, I was able to think about how I would make a pivot as an entrepreneur, I learned more about myself, and I understood the ease of a work-life balance. What does a work-life balance look like for you? What changes will you have to make?

Notes
CHAPTER 7

CHAPTER 8

Set Up Systems

Having a system for your business diminishes the weighed-down feeling one can experience with having a business. It is about setting things in order from having a plan, and strategy to building a team and procedures. I know you hear people talk about this and integrating a system that works for you is where you start.

There are various systems to set up such as time management skills, working with a schedule, technological systems, automation, and the list goes on. Ask yourself, what you need to put in place to help balance out your world. There are two different systems one can put in place, both are practical and automated. As for your personal life, the practical thing you can do is first manage your time wisely. We all like to live in the moment, but how would you like to live in the moment while managing time? Sounds crazy right? You do it by staying on task.

Don't put off tomorrow what you can do today, such a popular saying, yet so true. Procrastination is a robber of time and destiny. The more you procrastinate the more you will find yourself burning both ends of the stick. I know about this too well because like with so many others, I too have allowed procrastination to creep in. Next thing you know, you're working overtime to meet deadlines, missing family engagements, and missing moments to live life. Time management is key to a work-life balance.

"PROCRASTINATION IS A ROBBER OF TIME AND DESTINY"

Schedule your business tasks as well as your family time and events. For example, I keep a crazy calendar. I keep my calendar and business calendar together. I do this because it's easier to manage one calendar at a time. But the goal is to manage the calendar. Another practical system is working smart and not hard. This goes a little deeper, but ask yourself, what causes you to be lazy?

How we feel and what we do is aligned. If you're not feeling your best you tend to retreat from everything healthy to do so but staying on task with your responsibilities as a parent, business owner, spouse, friend, and even an employee can be jeopardized. Retreating to focus and return to your tasks refreshed enables you to not miss the moments. I say this because, in hard times, that's what we do, we retreat, and in most cases, it's not in a healthy way. It's avoidance, a way to not deal with the reality at hand.

I found myself in that place when pulling the pieces of my life together during those two years. I admit, there were things I didn't want to face or deal with. I didn't open my mail, read emails, nothing. When we retreat because of not wanting to cope, we lock ourselves up internally.

As for your business. Automation and outsourcing where you can be some of the best practices an entrepreneur can adopt. Ultimately, you want to develop a plan for your business to include marketing and branding. When properly planning your business out keeps you on track without having to redo something or spend more money.

Most of us don't vacation without planning, so why start or run a business without a plan? Proactiveness is better than being reactive. Also, make the best of your downtime. Some people like to take a social media break or what about those nights when you can't sleep? Those are opportunities you can take to maximize your time productively versus just scrolling through your social media platforms.

When I started to consider the plans to restart my business, I knew I had to increase my systems to perform better than before. When you go through something traumatic having ways to better function without touching a delicate part of your thinking into a spin is essential.

Although I was striving to begin again, I still did not feel like my optimum self. Something was missing. Being able to flow within boundaries and parameters helps me. Discipline balances everything in this chapter and your life. Master your time so it will not master you.

CHAPTER 9

Ignore The Noise

Many inner and exterior aspects keep an entrepreneur from attaining mental well-being. Internally, you're basking in your thoughts of defeat, self-doubt, second-guessing yourself asking if you are even worth it. The added pressure of wanting to succeed, provide for your children, or even become the first business owner in your family is enough. All these things add up in a mental bank account. You have a dream or vision you want to attain, and what you see in front if you don't match the dream of a peaceful entrepreneurial journey

Now, what do I mean by ignoring the noise? Ignore the naysayers and your competition. People are going to be people. If you are in an environment where there is only negative talk around or against you, you must be at a place of contentment and rise above it all. Avoid being like the "Jones" yes, the "Jones" of the business world.

Other entrepreneurs will succeed around you and with social media, many of them boast about their success. You tend to look at your endeavor as if you can't make it because you are not gaining the 6 or 7 figures. I'll be the first to be real with you, those who are talking about what they made, but what did they take to the bank as profits? Plenty of business owners have a large number of expenses that will bring down their bottom line.

Overall, it's ok. Remember what blessing is for them is for them and you have your own. Strategies and struggles are different. Some have a team and others don't. Focus and bring in alignment your goals and action steps for your business.

Entrepreneurship is risky. To be an entrepreneur means someone who takes a risk in embarking on your venture. The risk itself is bigger than we think. To manage a business and have a life means you will jeopardize so much that some have been in danger of losing friends, family members, and time.

Trust yourself, your idea, and the purpose you have in this world. Know what you want and go after it. Follow the steps that will keep building the staircase for you to rise to the highest height. Build from there and aspire to attain the uppermost level for your enterprise. Clear the chatter in your head and your surroundings.

CHAPTER 10

Prioritize Self-Care

How do you prioritize self-care? What does that look like to you? I have a 3R Method when it comes to taking care of my mental health. There comes a time when we should make time to Refresh, Recharge, and Regroup.

It is easy to get swept away mentally thinking about the next plan, getting children to school, having to spend time with your spouse/significant other or even just spending time with friends and family.

How many of us have been there?

My 3R Method is simple three words: REFRESH, RECHARGE, and REGROUP.
Your mind can go a million miles a minute, time traveling back and forth with thoughts of the past and future; when the present is where you are to focus on. How do you refresh, recharge, and regroup? Take a moment to think about it and write it down.

Refresh_____
_____

Recharge_____
_____

Regroup_____
_____

Refresh is necessary for your mind, body, and spirit. The waves of life will toss you back and forth. It means to stop and breathe. You are the one who controls the whirlwind in life. Just stop long enough to quiet your mind and your soul. Pray and meditate with breathing exercises. Light a candle, get a refreshing glass of wine, a good meal, or your favorite dessert. This is what I do, I allow myself to get lost in a peaceful indulging of goodness.

For some people, it's going for a long drive or sitting at the beach tuning into nature's melodies. A refresher helps to center you and your thoughts. Finding a positive outlet is key. My outlet is the gym and the beach. And during the pandemic was TikTok. Yes, I found my creative vibe on TikTok. The complexity of our mind is filled with imagination and thoughts. If the negative thoughts and ill imagination are not harnessed and healed, some can find themselves on a deep track of depression.

Recharge! Just like an overworked battery in your car needs to recharge, so do you. Take a break. It's ok to step away from the norm of entrepreneurial life. If you have already implemented time management, a system, and so forth; schedule a day or a weekend off. Be determined not to touch work at all. Even on your job, as an employee, take your personal or vacation time. Plan it and RECHARGE. To recharge a dead car battery, it is better to unhook it from the car to charge it. We aren't any different from that car battery. When you are recharged, you can think more clearly, operate more efficiently, and feel good mentally and physically.

REFRESH! RECHARGE! REGROUP!

Regroup! Once you refresh and recharge you can regroup. You come back to your business, job, and family ready to take on new tasks. You can effectively lead your business and your team. Thinking on your feet and making sound decisions come with a clear mind. I often think that if I had a clearer mind during the pandemic challenges, I would have been more resourceful versus taking on a 9-5.

Let's go back to the beginning of this chapter, think about what you wrote down about the ways you refresh, recharge, and regroup. Is there anything that you would do differently? Self-care comes n many forms and it's your responsibility to care for the only mind, body, and spirit you will have in this life. The journey you are on is for you. To fulfill it is to maintain a healthy mental and physical well-being.

After I regrouped, I was able to relaunch my business with a twist. I had a clear mind about my next steps, becoming the face of my brand, and leading my business from the front and not from my comfort zone. I embraced the change the pandemic offered me. After relaunching my business at the end of 2021, I look back and see the pandemic as a cocoon shielding me through time only to rebirth me as this beautiful butterfly. In writing this book and sharing my story, I want to bring awareness of mental health and entrepreneurship from an entrepreneur's perspective. To let every reader, know that they are not alone and it's possible to avoid or recover from burnout.

Vernica Williams, founder of ReClaiming Your Voice Podcast stated, "As a new entrepreneur, I have learned quickly, keeping your mental health in a healthy place is a non-negotiable expression of self-love. I honor the journey of my why."

Notes
CHAPTER 10

Notes

www.ingramcontent.com/pod-product-compliance
Lightning Source LLC
Chambersburg PA
CBHW080913170426
43201CB00017B/2317